The Children of Africville

Christine Welldon

NIMBUS PUBLISHING

Nimbus Publishing Limited
PO Box 9166,
Halifax, NS B3K 5M8
(902) 455-4286
www.nimbus.ca

Printed and bound in Canada

Cover & Book Design: Andrew Herygers

Library and Archives Canada Cataloguing in Publication

    Welldon, Christine
    The children of Africville / Christine Welldon.
    ISBN 978-1-55109-723-7

1. Africville (Halifax, N.S.)—Juvenile literature. 2. Black Canadians—Nova Scotia—Halifax—Social conditions—Juvenile literature. I. Title.

FC2346.9.B6W46 2009   j971.6'22500496   C2009-902862-X

NOVA SCOTIA
Tourism, Culture and Heritage

We acknowledge the financial support of the Government of Canada through the Book Publishing Industry Development Program (BPIDP) and the Canada Council, and of the Province of Nova Scotia through the Department of Tourism, Culture and Heritage for our publishing activities.

for Wilfred Welldon

~~~~~~

We are Africville

We are the little children who lie in the grass back the
field daydreaming as clouds dance overhead…

—Irvine Carvery

~~~~~~

Table of Contents

How the People Came to Africville

If you ever play on the beach, you will see some treasures in the sand. You may see sand dollars, maybe a toy, or a bottle pushed onto the beach by the waves. These are treasures the tide has left behind. You may watch the tide go out and pull some treasures back out to sea. Migration is like this. People feel the pushes and pulls that tell them to look for a better place to live. The push might come from hard times in the place where they live. The pull might be from the country or town where they want to migrate, so that they can find better lives for themselves.

It is this push and pull that has helped to make Canada what it is today, a nation of people from different places, living side by side like the patterns in a lovely, colourful quilt. Many of the people of different races and heritage in Canada came here because they were looking for a better way of life. Perhaps your parents or grandparents came to Canada for the same reason. All came with their hopes and dreams.

The children of Africville will tell you their story soon. But let's go back in time, long before they were born. That was when the black Canadians first came to Canada. They felt the pull of a better life. They wanted to escape from slavery. Many settled in Nova Scotia. They came to Hammonds Plains and Preston, cleared some land and built houses before the cold winter.

Many of the people of different races and heritage in Canada came here because they were looking for a better way of life. Perhaps your parents or grandparents came to Canada for the same reason. All came with their hopes and dreams.

The black Canadians worked hard to survive their first winter in Nova Scotia. They tried to become farmers, but found that the land was too rocky. They could not grow vegetables or keep animals on such poor land. Some had to become slaves again in Nova Scotia. They were hungry and poor. They had to sell themselves and their children as workers so they would

An aerial view of Africville, with North End Halifax in the background

have food and a place to live. When slavery ended, many felt the push to move away from the poor land. There was a pull to find a better place to live and work. Some migrated to big cities like Toronto or Montreal. Others migrated to Jamaica, Africa, the United States, or other parts of Nova Scotia.

For some, Bedford Basin at the edge of Halifax was a good place to settle. The land was not good for farming, but the people there were close to the city and could get jobs there. They could catch fish from their neighbour, the sea.

Two of the black men worked and saved some money to buy land in Nova Scotia. Their names were William Brown and William Arnold. In 1848, these two men bought five hectares of land in Halifax right on the waterfront of Bedford Basin. Many black settlers came to live on the land with them. They called this place Africville.

Bedford Basin is a large bay that forms the northwestern end of Halifax Harbour. It's about eight kilometres long and five kilometres wide.

Growing Up in Africville

The children of Africville did not grow up in a community where everyone locked their doors and no one knew their neighbours. They grew up in a very special community. Irvine Carvery was one of those children. Africville was a place that gave him a feeling of belonging. It was a place where he felt safe. He knew everyone, and everyone knew him. He likes to tell a story about this.

Children picking blueberries, with railway tracks, houses, and Bedford Basin behind them

"I was picking blueberries like we always did in the summer. I used an old glass milk bottle. Well, I tripped and fell on it and I had severe cuts. But I didn't have to run all the way back home. The very first house I went in, they tended to me till I could go to hospital for stitches." Irvine knew that people in his community looked out for one another. "We needed each other's help and someone was always there to help out."

Irvine was born in Africville in 1951. He lived "up the track," close to the railroad track that went through Africville. The tracks cut through the community and the trains made a lot of noise as they roared

Cyclists beside the railroad tracks

The Children of Africville

through, taking goods to other parts of Nova Scotia.

There were eighty families living in Africville, and Irvine came to know every family there. He went to school along with Terry Dixon. Terry had three sisters, and he was related to a famous boxer named George Dixon. Bernice Byers went to school with Irvine, too. Her family's house was "around the turn," near the bend of the railroad tracks. She had three brothers and a sister, a pet hen named Nelly, and a dog named Netty. Her best friends were Linda and Brenda. Bernice's nickname was Star, because she had sparkling eyes. She still does.

One day, someone stole Nelly. Bernice thinks they stole the hen because they were hungry. They cooked it and tried to eat it, but the bird was too tough so they threw the leftovers away. Bernice laughs about it now, but

Many people living in towns and cities used to keep hens as pets. Chickens help gardens by eating harmful bugs like grubs and aphids, and their fresh eggs are delicious.

Irvine, Terry, and Bernice were children who lived in a community where everyone knew them, and they knew everyone who lived there.

back then it was sad to see Nelly's orange feathers on the ground.

Irvine, Terry, and Bernice were children who lived in a community where everyone knew them, and they knew everyone who lived there. They spent their time like children in any other community in Canada. They went to school, did chores, and played with friends. But they had different experiences, too.

Doing Without

Two boys lifting the cover of a well

The Children of Africville

Africville homes, with a well and a nearby sign reading, "Please boil this water before drinking and cooking."

Think about your community. It may have stores, a hospital, a police station, and other services. Irvine, Terry, and Bernice lived in a community that did not have these things. They lived in a place where there were no inside toilets or running water. The water came from community wells, and Irvine went to the well every day to fetch water for his family. The water was not always safe to drink. Sometimes water that families used for drinking or cooking had to be boiled first to make it safe. Some wells had good water.

"My favourite drink was a glass of fresh, clear, cold water from the well," says Bernice. "To this day, I don't like to drink tap water. It's not the same as that well water."

The homes in Africville did not have central heating. People had wood stoves for cooking and heating. "We would start the fires in the morning," Bernice says. "My father trained us to do it right. Our first house burned down

Child on an Africville road

when I was a little girl. I had a scorch mark on my face from that fire. We were real careful after that."

Africville had no fire department and no fire hydrants. The government said there was too much rock in the ground to pipe the water in. The Africville people knew this was not true. They knew the government could pipe in the water if they cared to. But they did not do this. When there was a fire in a house, the house would burn down quickly. The fire department could not help if there were no fire hydrants.

Other people in Halifax had central heating in their homes and running water that was safe to drink. Other people had paved roads, and garbage pick-up. Africville did not have paved roads. It did not have garbage pick-up, or snowplow services. There was one very long road leading from Africville into the city of Halifax. Terry remembers this. "The men had to shovel the snow off this road in the winter. No one sent a snowplow into Africville to help keep the roads clear." The older children had a long walk up this road to school in Halifax. They did not have a school bus to take them.

Some houses in the winter

"Our school was always open. They didn't have teachers' days, like today," Bernice says. "When it snowed, we had to walk to school anyway, up the big hill. No snowplows. The snow was up to our waists sometimes."

Africville did not have a police station. It was a part of the city of Halifax, but Africville did not have any of these things. The people of Africville paid their taxes. They asked for all the things that they needed, but the government in Halifax did not give them what they asked for.

Sharing and Caring

The children of Africville could go to anyone if they needed help. That is how close everyone was. "The doors were always open," says Bernice. "If you were hungry, you could always get something to eat wherever you went." There were some very fine houses in Africville. There were also houses that were not so fine, where people lived who did not have much money. The

A family in their living room

people learned how to care for each other because work was sometimes hard to get. They never knew when they would need extra food or help, so they shared with each other when times were hard.

The people learned how to care for each other...they shared with each other when times were hard.

The children learned to share the way their parents told them. Irvine tells about this. "If we didn't help an old person to carry groceries, we'd hear about it. My father would fish in Bedford Basin. He'd get us to go around and sell fish. He told us that if we got to someone that didn't have any money, leave a couple of fish for them. You never knew when you would be the one without. The people always helped each other through hard times."

Matilda Newman's store

A Place to Meet

Everyone in Africville went to the Seaview African United Baptist Church on Sundays and sometimes on other days of the week, too. The church was a place for weddings, baptisms, and funerals. Bernice went to a church in Halifax, and she also went to the Africville church. It was the place to be if you wanted to worship and feel joy and happiness and celebrate that you lived with all the people you loved. It was a place to share your troubles, too. It was a place to meet each other and feel proud to be living in Africville. There was so much gospel singing and even dancing in the church, it was a sight to see.

At Easter, there was a sunrise service. Parents woke their children early, before five o'clock in the morning. "Wake up!" they would say. "Put on your best clothes. It's time for church." The families went to church as the sun began to rise. The children made sure their socks were clean and their clothes were pressed for this special Easter service.

People from other parts of the city liked to come to the Africville church. If you have heard soul music today, you will know what the gospel music was like in the Africville church.

Fun and Chores

Irvine and the children he played with were too young to know that they had less than others. They only knew that

> Gospel music is written and performed to express and celebrate a person or group's Christian beliefs. It is a very popular form of music, and it is performed in kitchens, churches, concert halls, and stadiums around the world.

Africville was their home and they were happy to be in this place.

For winter fun, the children would go sledding down the hills. Sometimes, when the moon was bright, they would sneak out of the house with their sleds. Irvine and his friends took some rope with them. "We'd put the heaviest kid on the first sled and tie the sleds together. When we went across the tracks, there were sparks everywhere!" Terry didn't have a sled of

Boys playing

his own. He and some friends made their own sled. This is how they did it: They found an old car that no one wanted anymore. They took off the hood, and turned it upside down. They went to the top of a hill and climbed inside, then slid down the hill. Terry had lots of fun this way.

Some houses, with snow on the ground

Irvine and his friends played hockey and skated. Bernice remembers her favourite place for skating. "Between the railway tracks and the shore there was a little creek. We used to skate on it when it froze in winter."

Because the homes in Africville did not have central heating, many houses were cold in winter. At bedtime, none of the children who shared a bed wanted to be the first into bed, because it was so cold. Wood-burning stoves helped families to stay warm. Irvine helped his brother to cut wood for the stove. He would sit on the log to hold it steady while his brother sawed it into firewood. Irvine and Terry, along with other children, picked up the chopped wood and carried it home to burn so their families would be warm in winter.

Terry had chores to do each day. "I went every day to fetch the water for cooking and cleaning," says Terry. "I pumped the well water into a silver bucket and took it home." He also helped his mother wash the dishes every day. Bernice helped her mother in the kitchen. She stood on a stool at the sink to wash the dishes. She helped with the washing and cleaning. "We couldn't go outside to play till we finished our chores."

Everyone in her family knew how to make bread, and she and her brothers took turns making it every day. One day, Bernice's father had a bad accident. He jumped on a train to take some coal to burn so his family could be warm. He fell off the train and lost an arm. It was hard for him to make the bread anymore, but he told his children how to do it.

In the summer, the children played by the waterfront of Bedford Basin. They saw whales swimming by.

The Children of Africville

Irvine and Terry liked to swim in the ocean, and fish from the pier. They caught mackerel, halibut, and even lobster. They balanced on floating logs or made rafts out of pieces of driftwood. Finding driftwood was one of Terry's favourite things to do. Irvine paddled his raft and imagined that he was the captain of a ship. Bernice made rafts with her girlfriends and floated on them.

> Driftwood is wood that has washed onto a shore. It can come from trees, houses that were swept into the ocean during storms, or even shipwrecks. Sometimes it acts as a shelter for birds and other animals.

The children picked the wild blueberries, raspberries, and pears that grew in the fields. "My favourite dessert was blueberry duff," says Bernice, "but I was scared of snakes. We had to look out for green snakes when we were picking berries in the blueberry patch." Bernice enjoyed dessert most of all. "My mother made the best gingerbread." Another favourite dessert was plum pudding. Her friend Linda had a grandmother who made the best plum pudding of anyone in Africville. Every Sunday,

> In the summer, the children played by the waterfront...they liked to play baseball, swim in the ocean, and fish from the pier.

Linda's grandmother made apple pie. It was so good that everyone wanted the recipe, but her grandmother did not give anyone the recipe. It was a secret.

On summer evenings, Irvine sat on the porch and listened to ghost stories that his big brother told him. Bernice liked to hear about haunted houses. If it was dark, she and her friends were scared to walk past a house called O'Brian's house. The children believed that if you walked past this house after midnight, you would be sure to see a ghost. Bernice walked past one

Children picking blueberries

The Children of Africville

time and saw a shadow in the window. She ran away from there as fast as she could.

Bedtime Stories

On long summer evenings, before bedtime, Irvine would listen to stories that his grandparents told. They were stories about the first people who came to Africville. Irvine's grandparents told him that when they were little, living in Africville was just like living in the country. You would never know that you were in a big city. They had pigs and chickens and goats back then. They would ride their horses through the farmlands.

Irvine's grandparents told him how some people in Africville got together and asked the city government of Halifax for a school. The government kept saying no. One day, at last, the city agreed to build a school, and soon the children went to school in their own community. The people of Africville were happy that they had not given up asking. But the school closed down just after Irvine was born. Then the children had to walk to Richmond School, outside their community.

A group of students

When the train tracks first came to Africville, the children had to be very careful, because they crossed the tracks every day. Irvine's parents and grandparents remembered a few people of Africville who were killed by trains. It was something the people had to live with. Irvine, Bernice, Terry, and their friends did not mind the noise of the trains. They invented fun games to play on the tracks. They would walk on the rails and try not to be the first to step on the ground. Sometimes they would line up bottles on the rails and try to hit them with rocks.

Irvine's parents told him that over the years, Africville grew in population. The city government put a toxic waste site very close to the Africville land. Toxic waste is garbage that can hurt people if they get close. The government also added a jail, a slaughterhouse, and other things that the Africville people did not want. Irvine and Terry walked past the jail every day on their way to school. Terry says, "I saw the prisoners planting potatoes. I waved to them and they waved back."

People walking on the railroad tracks

Irvine's parents said that many years ago, before Irvine was born, a ship exploded in the Halifax Harbour. The explosion damaged buildings and houses in Halifax and some in Africville. The government gave the people of Halifax money to fix the damage to their houses. They did not give money to the people of Africville. The Africville people carried on and rebuilt their own homes without help from the city government.

The Halifax Explosion happened on December 6, 1917. It was caused by two ships, the Belgian *Imo* and the French *Mont Blanc*, colliding with each other in the harbour. Over two thousand people died and over nine thousand were injured. It is still the world's largest accidental explosion caused by humans.

Irvine listened to these stories. He heard about the big fire that happened in Africville a few years before he was born. So many houses burned because the Halifax Fire Department did not come to Africville. They would not give the people of Africville waterlines for fire hydrants. He heard about how the government people wanted to tear down Africville back then. They blamed the people of Africville for the fire and all their other troubles. The city of Halifax was growing and there was talk of how the government needed more land and might want to

Laundry drying in the breeze by the water

take Africville land. No one in Africville believed that they might lose their land.

Skin Deep

You may have felt racial prejudice from other children. You may have a feeling of racial prejudice about others. Racial prejudice is an attitude others have when they do not like the colour of your skin. People with racial prejudice do not care if you are a good person. The only thing they judge you on is the way you look.

Some Africville children felt this prejudice when they went outside their community to Richmond School. For

People with racial prejudice do not care if you are a good person. The only thing they judge you on is the way you look.

many years, black children were segregated. They went to schools for only black children. But around the time Irvine, Terry, and Bernice were born, the government began to integrate the children in school. Irvine went to a school where black and white children were in classes together. This was a way to stop prejudice against black and white children learning together.

Some teachers believed that children from Africville were slow to learn even though this was not true. This is racial prejudice. Teachers sometimes put children in the "slow" class. The teachers believed that Africville children were not able to learn as fast as white children. This made some black children feel bad about themselves, and they did not want to go to school. Many Africville children did not reach grade six because of the prejudice against them.

Terry went to a school called Mulgrave Park. It was outside Africville. He was a good student and liked school. He did not feel racial prejudice at his school when he was very young. He had many friends and worked hard. When he was older, he began to notice racial prejudice. He says that white kids came to the edge of the hill above Africville, threw rocks into the community, and shouted mean words.

Children playing on a swing set

Bernice made a lot of friends at her school. She was happy to go to school and worked hard to succeed. "I wasn't afraid of anyone," she says. "Sometimes I was a terror at school. If anyone said something to me that I didn't like, I'd chase them. One time, I chased Brenda all the way home with a shoe in my hand. We made up and we've been best friends ever since."

Children playing with dolls in a garden

Irvine felt racial prejudice in and outside of school. "We used to come in town with our parents shopping— you could feel it, the tension. When you went to school the white kids would call you names, teachers treated you different."

Irvine's teacher did not allow the black children to take books home from school. The teacher thought the Africville children would lose the books. Irvine liked to take his favourite book outside at recess time to read. That was all the teacher would let him do to get extra reading time. Some children were not learning very much because of this racial prejudice, but their parents

The Children of Africville

told them to keep going to school and not to give up. They said that the way to success was through education.

Troubles

Many of the families in Africville had lived there for a long time. They were proud to live in the community. Africville was growing. There were more children being born and growing up there. When they grew up, they wanted land of their own. Their parents gave them some of the family land. Soon, more people were living on smaller chunks of land.

Two children near Seaview African United Baptist Church

After some years, there was not enough land for everyone. Worse, there were people called squatters who came from the city. These people were not related to the Africville people. They lived on the land without paying rent. The community became even more crowded.

Africville was crowded with people and there was not enough land for them.

A Dump Comes to Africville

The city government decided to put a garbage dump right at the edge of Africville. Now, rats came to the dump to look for food. The government did not care that all this would be bad for the health of the community.

Many children liked to look for interesting things at the dump. Bernice and her friends looked for treasures there. "It was like a gold mine. You could find pretty glass bottles, bits of metal."

Terry's mom told him not to go near the dump, but he broke the rules. He used to go with his friends to look

The Halifax city dump, with Seaview African United Baptist Church and some houses in the background

for things. Terry laughs when he tells this story. "We found some things that were better than we had at home. One day, a truck full of broken toys came to the dump. That was a good day for us. My mother knew I was going to the dump even though she told me not to go. She told me to pull my socks up over my pants while I was there to stop the rats from running up my legs."

Candy trucks came to the dump, too. They dropped boxes of candy that were too old to sell. The children were happy when this happened. They had all the candy they could eat. The fruit and vegetable truck would drop cases of things like oranges and bananas that were in good shape. The children took home everything they could carry.

The people of Africville did not want the dump in their community. They did not

Dumps, also called landfills (and middens, if you're talking about long ago), have been used all over the world. But poorly managed dumps can cause problems for people who live nearby; they can be smelly, dangerous, and can attract all kinds of rodents, like rats (which can carry diseases).

Africville houses in the autumn, viewed from the edge of the city dump

feel they had the power to fight against the dump. It was a problem that they had to live with. Some looked for items in the dump that could help them. It was against the law to take things from the dump, but there were some Africville people who did not have very much money. These people found many treasures in the dump that they could sell for money to support their families. They found scrap metal that they could sell. There were nails, and paint, and sometimes furniture that they could fix up. They found clothing that was still good. The women washed it and sewed it to make good

The Children of Africville

clothes for their families. They found wood that they could burn to keep warm in winter.

Most of the Africville grown-ups did not take things from the dump. They were angry that it was so close to their homes, and that when people talked about Africville, they talked about the dump at the same time. The Africville people wanted the city government to let them start a salvage company for the men who had no jobs. These men could have the right to sell things from the dump and earn money. But the government did not agree to do this for Africville. It did put an incinerator beside the dump, to burn the garbage and keep the rats away.

Leaving Africville

THE MAIL-STAR

HALIFAX, NOVA SCOTIA, CANADA   JUNE 6, 1963

Africville Problem Getting City's Attention

THE MAIL-STAR

HALIFAX, NOVA SCOTIA, CANADA   JANUARY 7, 1964

City to Make Africville Move as Painless as Possible

HE MAIL-STAR

...OTIA, CANADA   MARCH 8, 1965

...gly Shacktown Going

THE MAIL-STAR

HALIFAX, NOVA SCOTIA, CANADA   JANUARY 3, 1966

Africville May Disappear by Year's End

THE MAIL-STAR

HALIFAX, NOVA SCOTIA, CANADA   JANUARY 3, 1966

Ghetto Going on Schedule

The children of Africville began to hear a new word when their parents were talking. The word was "relocation." Relocation meant that the people would have to move away from Africville. The community of Africville had a strong culture. It had a history that its people shared. It had stories and music that they all knew. It had traditions or a way of life that everyone

Children walking on a pathway with the Bedford Basin in the background

understood. The black people had gone through many hard times together as they built their community. No one wanted to leave Africville, but the government in Halifax gave reasons why the people should relocate. The people in the government did not know or care that it had a strong culture. They said that Africville was a slum. They said it was embarrassing to have a place like Africville in their city. The people of Africville said their community was not a slum. They took care of their houses. They paid their taxes. They were proud of the community.

A family together in the living room

The Children of Africville

The government people said they wanted to use the land for other things. They wanted to build an expressway on the land. They said black people should not live separately from other people. They should be moved to houses with safe water to drink, and indoor toilets.

Irvine, Terry, and other children like them were excited about moving. It was a new adventure. But older people in Africville were very unhappy. They had lived in Africville all their lives. Their family and friends were here. It was cheap to live here. How could they afford to live in better houses?

The people in the government did not understand that

Tax is money paid by citizens and companies to the government. There are many different kinds of taxes; sales tax is added to items you buy, and income tax is taken from money you earn. There is also a kind of tax called "property tax," which people pay the municipal government. The municipal government is supposed to use the money it collects to pay for water and sewage services, garbage pick-up, electricity, roads, snowplowing, and other services for the people who pay the taxes.

A young boy standing in a garden

Africville was not just a bunch of houses. Africville was much more than that. In Africville, there were stories and songs to share about hard times and happy times. There was pride and caring for each other. There was a history they shared that reached back for over one hundred

The people of Africville felt strong together. How would they be strong if they no longer lived in Africville?

A Halifax city official talking to Africville residents

The Children of Africville

years. The people of Africville felt strong together. How would they be strong if they no longer lived in Africville?

Yes or No?

The children saw strangers in the community talking to their parents. They saw their parents looking very worried. The strangers were from the city government and they talked to their parents about relocating. The government people

Participants at a meeting at the Seaview African United Baptist Church

asked their parents if they would take money to move away from Africville.

Some of the people said yes. These were people who were young and wanted a new life. Other people said yes because they had not lived in Africville for very long and they did not own houses or land. But some of the people

Some younger participants at a public meeting at the church

said no. These were people who had lived in Africville all their lives and owned houses or land.

The people from the city government did not give up. They held meetings in the Africville church and asked the people of Africville to come to the meetings. Some went to the meetings. Many did not go. They gave up. They did not want to fight the relocation because they did not think they could win.

Some parents had their own meetings, too. They

The Children of Africville

tried to think of ways to stop the relocation. They had always asked for water to be piped in, and for police and fire protection, but did not get them. Now they asked the city government to help rebuild Africville with all these things, so they would not have to relocate. The city government said no.

There was a very important meeting at the church. The people of Africville had to vote yes or

Participants speaking at a public meeting at Seaview African United Baptist Church

no on the relocation. By this time, the people did not have any hope that they could stay in the community they loved. There were four hundred people living in Africville, but only forty-one people from Africville voted at that meeting. Thirty-seven voted for relocation. Most of the people did not go to the meeting and did not vote. They just gave up.

People from the government spoke to every family

about how much money they would get to move away from Africville. The government gave some families more than others because some families had a deed to their land or home. They had papers to prove they owned the land or the house. Other families were renting their homes and did not have deeds. These people were not given very much money. Still others were squatting, living in very poor sheds. These people did not own land or pay rent. They did not receive any money for moving away.

Bulldozers and Dump Trucks

When families received their money, a city truck came to move their things. The people were not happy to see that their things were being moved in city dump trucks. Many families had very fine furniture. It was hard to watch their good furniture carried into a dump truck. It was harder still to move to a new place with your things in a dump truck that all the new neighbours could see.

The Children of Africville

As soon as a family moved, bulldozers came to tear down their house. Terry was twelve years old when he saw the bulldozers come into Africville. He says, "I didn't understand what was happening. But when I saw the bulldozers

Dorothy Carvery's belongings being moved in a City of Halifax dump truck

hit a house where I used to play, the whole house just fell down. It hurt to see that. I felt empty." Terry's family owned their house. His mother was careful to get the best deal she could. She knew she could not stop the relocation.

HE
CANADA
icvi
/'s /
on the beach,
TA
Goi
terfront of Be
black settlers
L-
pear

A young boy in front of a house that would soon be torn down

When the children and their parents saw bull-dozers knocking down a house, they felt very sad. They knew that it was no good to fight relocation. It was like seeing a bully come to boss them around and they could not stop the bully.

Irvine remembers this time. "They tore down people's homes before people could leave them," Irvine says. "There was one man, they tore his house down while he was in the hospital. He didn't have any place to go when he came out of hospital. Another family was in

Toronto, visiting. When they came back, they found that they had lost everything, all their pictures that told their history, everything was lost."

Halifax city officials in Africville

Irvine remembers a friend's grandmother. She told the city men that she would not move. She wanted more money for her house. Her neighbours had moved out and bulldozers had torn down their homes. When they did this, they damaged the well. This woman could not get water to drink. The city gave her a tank of water. In the winter, the water froze. When this happened, of course she did not have water to drink. She gave up and took the money and moved. The fire department used her empty house to train their firefighters. They burned her house down.

Then something happened that told everyone Africville was finished. The bulldozers tore down the Africville church. Without the church, the people could

not meet to pray, share their problems, or celebrate being together. Terry remembers this day. "The worst thing was waking up one morning, we looked outside, the church was gone," says Terry. "Then we understood our community was over because the one building that gave life to our community was gone, the heart was gone. It was so empty now. We moved soon after. Lots of people moved after they tore down the church."

Seaview African United Baptist Church before its destruction

Without the church, the people could not meet to pray, share their problems, or celebrate being together. The city government of Halifax paid money for the church that they tore down. The Africville people put the money into a fund to help pay for their children's education.

The Children of Africville

A Brave Man Says No

The last person who lived in Africville kept saying no when he was offered money for his house. His house was in an important place. The city government wanted to build a bridge and his house was in the way. The government could not finish the bridge until this man left. His name was Aaron "Pa" Carvery.

Bernice, Irvine, and Terry all remember Pa Carvery, because he had lived all his life in Africville. Pa's grandfather came to Nova Scotia to escape slavery in the United States. His father was born in Africville and died there. Pa

Aaron "Pa" Carvery

Carvery was a grey-haired old man at this time. He was a coal handler on the Halifax waterfront. He was a very strong man and had scars on his hands and arms from the hard work he did all through his life. He was very strong inside, too.

The city tried to give Pa Carvery a suitcase of money.

He would not take the money. He had dignity and pride. He stayed on when all the houses around him were torn down. He did not want to give up. The government told him he had not ever paid his taxes, but Pa Carvery knew this was not true. He had kept copies of all the taxes he had paid. He showed these copies to them.

Slavery is a practice in which some people are forced to work for other people, no matter how badly they are treated. After slavery stopped being legal in Nova Scotia, many slaves fled there from the United States so that they could be free. Slavery is a terrible practice, but it still exists in some parts of the world.

The government offered Pa Carvery a little more money, but not the sum he wanted. The government said if he didn't take the money, they would take his land anyway. Pa Carvery knew he had to give up. He took the money and moved into a rooming house. He always felt sad that he could no longer live in Africville, the place he loved.

The Children of Africville

A New Place to Live

Irvine was fifteen when his family's house was bull-dozed. He and his family moved into the city to a house in Uniacke Square. Bernice and her family moved to a neighbourhood called Mulgrave Park. Terry's family moved there, too.

Bernice says, "It was all concrete, now. I missed trees, the water, and picking berries." Irvine, Terry, and Bernice still had friends in the new community who had moved from Africville.

Terry remembers the first day his family moved into their new house. Terry was excited that he did not have to fetch water from a well anymore. "We ran up and down the stairs and turned on all the taps. It was hard to believe that now we had running water inside our house. We played with the taps like they were a toy!"

They did not have to fetch wood for the stove. Now they had central heating. There were no more fights about who went to bed first to warm up the bed. They were always warm in their new home.

It was Halloween when Terry's family moved. "We made ghost costumes with sheets, and went around the houses in

the new neighbourhood. We couldn't go very far; it was too big. But we got some candies and treats."

But now there were rules to follow that the children

They could not shout a hello to people who passed, the way they did in Africville. They could not pick berries, fish in the sea, or swim.

were not used to. They could no longer sit on the steps outside their new homes and share stories. They could not shout a hello to people who passed, the way they did in Africville. They could not pick berries, fish in the sea, or swim. They did not live so near the ocean. They were more cut off from each other. Their old community was torn apart. They did not feel that they belonged in this new community.

Some people from Africville had to move into very poor homes in Halifax. Good houses were not ready for them. These people now lived in places that were in a bad state, much worse than any place in Africville.

Many parents owned their own homes when they lived in Africville. Now they had to borrow money from the bank to pay for their new houses. Some lost their new homes because they did not earn enough money to pay for them.

Some neighbours had racial prejudice against the people from Africville. The white neighbours did not want them in their community. They did not welcome the Africville people. Terry remembers this. "I could not get up, go outside, and see friends and family close by, see the Africville people. I didn't have that feeling that every house is safe. I couldn't run to any house if I was in trouble, ask for help, or get a bandage put on a cut. Now I was with people I didn't know and who didn't know me. The white kids didn't want to know me."

The people of Africville had always been kind to each other. They always let people stay with them, even if they were not related. Now they could not do this. It cost too much money. The government gave them some money to help them start their new lives, but this was not enough.

But more families were happy with their new homes. Now the people had all the services that they did not have in Africville. They had water and sewer services, and police and fire protection. Even though it was hard at first, they made their new lives a success.

Broken Promises

The government told the Africville people that they could get some training for new jobs in the city. Some people did not have the education to learn new skills. Many tried to learn new skills but it was very hard for them. The government did not help. They did not write down their promise to help with job skills, so they forgot the people of Africville. The people had to do the best they could.

A small group of people from Africville formed a committee to push for more help. They called it the Africville Action Committee. They asked for money for the Africville people who needed help to keep their new homes. The committee wrote letters to the newspapers. It met with the mayor of Halifax. The committee did not get the money it asked for. It did get some job training for people. The members of the committee also held a meeting to remember Africville. Hundreds of Africville people came together for this event.

The Children of Africville

CHAPTER THREE

Not Just a Memory

57

Today the place where Africville stood is called Seaview Memorial Park. It is only a field now, but Bernice, Irvine, Terry, and other people who grew up there know where their houses were. They know where the school playground was, and the church. They know the places where they fished and swam and played. It may be only an empty place, but the spirit of the Africville community is there. When they visit this place and smell the salt air, feel the ocean breezes, they imagine they can hear the music and singing from the old Africville church. They can almost hear the happy sounds of the Africville children playing tag or building rafts.

Africville was torn down many years ago. By 1970, all the houses were gone. The city did not use the land. Irvine, Terry, and Bernice are

> When they visit this place and smell the salt air, feel the ocean breezes, they imagine they can hear the music and singing from the old Africville church.

The last Africville house to be torn down

grown up now with families of their own. Their children do not know what it was like to grow up in Africville and belong to a community of people who have the same ancestors.

Irvine felt sad that his children would not grow up like this. Africville and its lessons were lost to them. "After I got married and started my own family, I realized what I had lost. My children will not enjoy the privilege that I enjoyed, knowing your family is around

The Children of Africville

you, being in a place where family is talked about every day."

Irvine knows about growing up with people who have pride in their heritage. "I knew who my people are, who my ancestors are. I always had the feeling that I'm somebody. I had a sense of belonging. My children won't enjoy that. Being children in Africville, we were the last to enjoy that."

Irvine decided that they must remember Africville and keep it alive in their hearts. They must remember the lesson

Irvine Carvery showing his children where Africville used to be

that if they do not work together to push for change, they will lose what they treasure. He and others see the Africville experience as a lesson for everyone to ask questions and stand firm.

Many others who were children in Africville also wanted to keep the memory and the lessons of Africville alive. Bernice and Irvine joined together with others who grew up in Africville. They did not see their old friends and neighbours very much after they were relocated. They decided to hold a special day for all the people from "out home" who had lived in Africville. They called it Acquaintance Day. Bernice, Irvine, and others helped to organize this important day. On this day, old friends and neighbours could meet again and talk about their memories.

They went back to the place where Africville used to be. They invited all of Africville's people to come to this place on Bedford Basin and talk about their lives in Africville. They wanted everyone to share stories, meet new children and old friends, and keep the spirit of Africville alive.

The Children of Africville

Being Strong Together

The people of Africville know that if they had been stronger as a team before relocation, they would have won a better place for themselves. Everyone agreed that the government people and the people of Africville had learned a lesson. The people of Africville promised each other they would never forget this lesson.

In 1991, the Government of Nova Scotia planned to build a road for big trucks on the Africville land. The black community used the lessons they had learned. They stood up and made a protest to stop these plans. They got what they wanted and stopped the truck road from being built.

Africville has a brave history and a strong culture that deserves respect.

One day, the Africville people met with the government people. They talked about why they lost their community. They said that it is important to work together as a team and push hard for a good deal. The government people agreed that they should have done a better job of listening to the Africville people. They should have given more help. They agreed that they did not know how important Africville was to its people. They understand now that Africville has a brave history and a strong culture that deserves respect.

Keeping the Memory Alive

Irvine and his team did not want anyone to forget Africville. They wondered how they could make sure of this. Their friend Deborah Dixon had a good idea. She asked her friends Linda and Brenda to help with this idea. Irvine and Bernice helped, too. Together as a team, they helped to create the Africville Genealogy Society. This team is making sure that everyone remembers Africville. They help the Africville people keep in touch with one another. The team plans a picnic every year in the place where Africville used to stand. Irvine is still working today for the community. He has won medals for his service. Irvine and Bernice and their friends Linda and Brenda became leaders to speak for the black community.

The team organized an exhibit at a university in

The Children of Africville

Halifax. Many people came to this exhibit. They heard the songs, looked at photographs, and listened to poetry about Africville. Visitors looked at china and linen from some Africville homes and there was even the pulpit from the Africville church to see. The team took the exhibit across Canada. They wanted everyone to know about Africville. They did not want anyone to forget their community.

A beautiful photograph showing Africville before it was torn down

All the Hot Dogs You Can Eat

Imagine a picnic with hundreds of people that you know. You can eat all the ice cream and hot dogs you want! You can play games or jump in the jumping castle.

This is what happens at the Africville picnic. Every year, in July, the people of Africville meet in Seaview Memorial Park, the place where Africville used to be. They bring campers and tents. The celebration lasts for the weekend. It is a time to catch up with each other, to share stories, and to have fun. The people meet and greet old friends from "out home," from Africville.

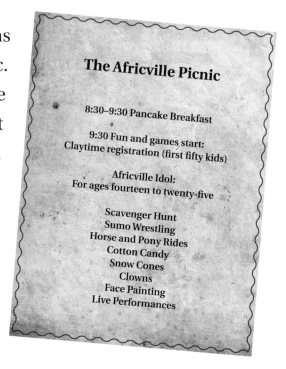

The Africville Picnic

8:30–9:30 Pancake Breakfast

9:30 Fun and games start:
Claytime registration (first fifty kids)

Africville Idol:
For ages fourteen to twenty-five

Scavenger Hunt
Sumo Wrestling
Horse and Pony Rides
Cotton Candy
Snow Cones
Clowns
Face Painting
Live Performances

Terry likes to go to the picnic and bring his children. He says sometimes it is painful to remember how things used to be and how much the Africville people have lost. "It is a painful kind of joy that I feel," he says. "For three days, we have our community back." He likes to stop and look at the train tracks, smell the salt water, hear the sound of the waves. These sights and sounds bring back the feeling of belonging for Terry.

Bernice and Irvine like to plan the games and contests for the children at the picnic. They have scavenger hunts, races, soccer games, and a jumping castle. There is good food and music and all the picnic food is free for the children. They can eat ice cream, hamburgers, and hot dogs and compete to be Africville Idol.

They meet to share their memories and celebrate their history. They meet to remember that they must always be strong together.

On Sunday, in a big canvas tent, the people sing the way they used to at the old Africville church. They meet to share their memories and celebrate their history and the joy of being together again. They meet to remember that they must always be strong.

Lessons of Africville

Irvine has not forgotten the lessons his people learned. He and his team asked the government to help build a church that looks the same as the old

> Terry hopes that all the children whose parents grew up in Africville... will remember their heritage and hold tight to their values.

Africville church. They asked for housing on Africville land. They want to open a centre on this land. The centre will have exhibits that tell the story of Africville.

Bernice believes that it is important to have this centre. "We want to build a replica of the Baptist church. We want to have a centre for tourists to visit, with activities for kids. We want to get our land back. It was ours. It was taken from us. We want to put a residence on the land for the old people who were children in Africville. We want to live on our land again." They are determined to get the changes they want. They know they can do it.

Terry knows that education is very important. He wants his children and others to go to college. He hopes that all the children whose parents grew up in Africville will learn the lessons, and learn to appreciate the value of Africville. He hopes they will remember their heritage and hold tight to their values.

The Children of Africville

Children playing in Africville before it was torn down

Bernice has good advice for children today. "If you go after nothing, you will get nothing. If you want it, go get it," she says. "The mind is a terrible thing to waste." Bernice lives this advice every day. She is a strong member of the team, raising funds and organizing events. She is a proud and hard-working woman.

Irvine goes to schools and universities to talk to students about Africville. He does not want anyone to forget his community. If you ask Irvine where he is from, he says proudly, "I am from Africville."

Some Famous People

Africville has many celebrities. These are people who did outstanding things with their lives.

Richard Preston was the pastor for the Africville church. He formed the first African Baptist Association in 1854.

George Dixon was born in Africville. He was the first black man to win the World Featherweight Championship for boxing, in 1896. He was the champion from 1896 to 1900.

Gordon T. C. Jemmott was a star hockey player, and he coached the Africville Brown Bomber hockey team. He was headmaster at the Africville school.

GEORGE DIXON.

George Dixon

The Children of Africville

Portia White was seventeen when she began teaching. She taught school in Africville for a while. She took singing lessons and entered contests. She won a silver cup at the Nova Scotia Music Festival and received a scholarship to study singing. Soon she was touring around the world and she even sang for Queen Elizabeth.

Portia White

Joe Sealey is a jazz musician. His father was born in Africville. Joe wrote music about Africville called "Africville Suite." There are many songs, poems, books, and even a film about Africville. All of these keep the memory of Africville alive.

A Timeline of Nova Scotia's Black History

1776 to 1784: The American War of Independence brings Black Loyalists into Nova Scotia.

1792 to 1796: Black Loyalists migrate to Sierra Leone in West Africa, leaving because of the hardships of settling in Nova Scotia.

1796 to 1800: The Maroons, from Jamaica, settle in East Preston as free blacks.

1800: The Maroons leave for Sierra Leone in West Africa because they are not happy with the conditions in Nova Scotia.

1810: By this year, 765 black slaves in Nova Scotia have been freed.

1813 to 1816: Two thousand black refugees come to Nova Scotia from the United States to escape slavery.

1815: The first pioneer village is settled in the Preston area, in September.

1820: Septimus Clarke, a black settler, is given fifty hectares of land. Forty-two other black settlers successfully receive land grants in Halifax County.

1827: The government stops giving land grants.

1842: Black settlers are given 730 hectares of land.

1848: William Brown and William Arnold buy land on Bedford Basin, to be known as Africville.

1849: The Africville Baptist Church is built, later called the Seaview African United Baptist Church.

1850s: Railroad tracks are laid through the community.

1851: By this time, 4,908 blacks are living in Nova Scotia. Africville people petition for a school teacher in Hammonds Plains.

1852: A community well is built in Africville.

1858: Sewage disposal pits are placed on the edge of Africville.

1870: George Dixon is born in Africville.

1872: An Africville resident teaches children in the church and later in a private home.

The Children of Africville

1883:	The first school is built in Africville.
1896 to 1900:	George Dixon wins the World Featherweight Championship for boxing.
1917:	The Halifax Explosion destroys many buildings in Halifax, including some in Africville.
1919:	Africville people petition for police service, but are unsuccessful.
1932 to 1935:	The Brown Bombers hockey team plays for Africville.
1933:	Gordon T. C. Jemmott, coach of the Brown Bombers, becomes the new headmaster at the Africville school. He holds this position for twenty-five years.
1935:	Africville people petition for water service with no success.
1939:	Africville people petition for a post office, street lights, and street numbers. They are successful.
1947:	A fire in Africville destroys seven homes. Government officials begin to talk about relocating the Africville people.

1951:	Irvine Carvery is born in Africville.
1953:	The Africville school is closed, and Africville children are integrated into Halifax schools.
1955:	The city dump is moved to within one hundred metres of the edge of Africville.
1957:	A fire in Africville claims the lives of three children.
1959:	A government survey to find out how residents feel about living in Africville is conducted.
1964:	On January 9, thirty-seven Africville residents vote for relocation.
1969:	The Africville Action Committee is formed.
1970:	Aaron "Pa" Carvery is the last Africville person to leave the community.
1972:	On Sunday, August 6, 1,200 people come back to the Africville site for a memorial service.

The Children of Africville

1982:	Acquaintance Day is organized by Deborah Dixon-Jones, Brenda Steed-Ross, and Linda Mantley.
1984:	The Africville Genealogy Society is formed by Deborah Dixon-Jones, Brenda Steed-Ross, and Linda Mantley.
1985:	Seaview Memorial Park opens on June 22.
1989:	The Africville Exhibition opens on October 20.
2002:	The former community of Africville is named a National Historic Site by the Government of Canada on July 15.

Acknowledgements

The author wishes to thank the Africville "children" and others, who were so helpful in the writing of this book: Bernice Byers-Arsenault, Hope Carvery, Irvine Carvery, Nelson Carvery, Stanley Carvery, Terry Dixon, Linda Mantley, Kathleen Odusanya, Brenda Steed-Ross, and Beatrice Wilkins. Thanks also to Ardith Pye, Rose Vaughan, and to Dr. Henry Bishop, Black Cultural Centre, Dartmouth.

Resources

Africville Genealogy Society. *The Spirit of Africville.* Halifax: Formac Publishing, 1992.

Clairmont, D. H., and D. W. Magill. *Africville: The Life and Death of a Canadian Black Community.* Revised edition. Toronto: Canadian Scholars Press, 1987.

Shades of Blue. Produced and directed by Susan Poizner. Mississauga: Marlin Motion Pictures, 2007.

Africville Lament

A nother time, another place

    But the memories are vivid and strong

F rom "BIG TOWN" to "AROUND THE TURN"

    We had a place to belong

R emember the closeness of neighbors and friends

    Our elders so greatly respected

I n our own small world, with such freedom and love

    Our unity kept us protected

C ity living was fine for others

    But our haven "OUR HOME" reigned above

V ery true, it is, that we had our faults

    But our foundation was built on love

I n days gone by, our village stood strong

    City politics led us astray

L et others learn from our misjudgments

    Trust never what "they say"

L et the young ones learn at what once was

    With pictures and tales of the land

E ach of us must teach them this

    "Don't let go of what's yours—Take a stand."

—Excerpted from a poem by Terry Dixon

The Children of Africville

Image Sources

Nova Scotia Archives and Records Management: front cover, 3, 5, 7, 8, 10, 11, 15, 22, 25, 29, 31, 33, 34, 39, 42, 43, 44, 45, 48, 49, 57, 70, 71

Black Cultural Centre: 12, 18, 19, 24, 27, 30, 41, 47, 51, 60, 61, 65, 69

Library and Archives Canada: 16, 40

Albert Lee: back cover, 57

Province of Nova Scotia: 13